The Tutor's Handbook
MATH
Grade 1

Written by Kimberly Seto and Alberto Lazaro

Illustrated by Patty McCloskey

Editor: Kathleen Hex
Introduction: Carol Wright
Book Design: Rita Hudson
Cover Design: Riley Wilkinson
Graphic Artist: Randy Shinsato
Cover Photos: Anthony Nex Photography

FS122129 The Tutor's Handbook: Math Grade 1
All rights reserved—Printed in the U.S.A.
23740 Hawthorne Blvd., Torrance, CA 90505

TABLE OF CONTENTS
Grade K-1

As a tutor for a young child, consider your role as that of a coach. Picture the coaches you have seen running along the sidelines at local soccer games. They believe in their teams. They encourage, support, advise, and challenge to help their teams achieve victory. As a tutor, you will assume a similar role as you help the child achieve success in first grade math activities.

Patience

Probably one of the most important qualities in a coach or tutor is patience. You have a clear understanding of the math concepts that you will be helping the child develop. However, the student will not master these skills overnight. Allow the child sufficient time to explore, practice, and develop each skill you present.

Enthusiasm

Just like an athletic coach, the tutor must convey to the student a belief in his or her ability to master the skills. Be an encourager! Call attention to the progress that the child is making in math. Your sincere praise will help the child feel comfortable with taking risks and may help him or her develop confidence with math activities.

Process

Soccer coaches are obviously focused on helping their teams win. If you look closely, you will notice that coaches actually spend much of the time helping the team learn how to win a game. As you help the student develop a variety of math strategies, try to focus a significant amount of energy on the things that the child is doing to solve the problems. Encourage the student to talk out loud as he or she thinks about and works on a problem. Pose thoughtful questions about the process used to solve a problem. This is more helpful than simply marking answers right or wrong.

Make it a common practice to ask the child to tell you how he or she got an answer to a problem. If you discover that the child began solving an addition problem in the tens place, ask the child why he or she started there. Just as the athletic coach does not allow the team to practice over and over the wrong way to play, help the student succeed by talking about the process that will help him or her reach the correct answer. Resist the temptation to simply tell your student the correct answer, as this will result in little long-term learning. Pose questions about the problem that will challenge the child to explore and use all of the different strategies that he or she is developing. When the child correctly solves a problem, encourage him or her to describe the process used to solve it. Ask the child to reiterate the steps used to arrive at the correct answer.

Be enthusiastic about learning!

In your important role of tutor as coach, have patience with your student! Remember that the child is learning as fast as he or she can. Be enthusiastic about learning! Your excitement and encouragement may help the child improve his or her attitude toward math. Finally, focus on the process of learning! It is just as important as getting the right answer.

The following is an outline of the skills that a student should have by the end of the first grade. These standards for instruction are set by the National Council of Teachers of Mathematics.

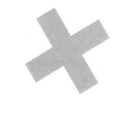

NUMBERS AND COMPUTATION
First graders should be able to

- count and read numbers to 100

- add and subtract one- and two-digit numbers to 20

- find the sum of three one-digit numbers

- use ordinal numbers from first to tenth

- understand place value of tens and ones

- compare and order numbers to 100

- use inverse relationships ($2 + 3 = 5$, $5 - 3 = 2$)

- make reasonable estimates in computation and comparisons of numbers

- understand simple fractions of a whole (1/2, 1/3, 1/4, 3/4)

GEOMETRY
First graders should be able to

- identify and describe two-dimensional shapes: square, triangle, rectangle, and circle

- recognize and identify lines of symmetry in shapes

- describe the relationship of objects to one another (near, far, above, below, up, down)

- identify and describe three-dimensional objects: sphere, cylinder, cone, pyramid

PATTERNS
First graders should be able to

- recognize, predict, and extend shape and number patterns

- compare numbers using *between, before,* and *after*

- skip count to 100 by 2, 5, and 10

- recognize and construct fact families for addition and subtraction

DATA ANALYSIS, STATISTICS, AND PROBABILITY
First graders should be able to

- use tables, patterns, and sequences to explore relationships

- understand the terms and symbols *greater than, less than,* and *equal to* (>, <, =)

- create number sets to 100

- collect, organize, display, and compare data in simple graphs and tables by using concrete objects, pictures, or numbers

- make comparisons by using information in graphs

- identify the probability of an event as *certain* or *impossible,* and as *more* or *less likely*

MEASUREMENT
First graders should be able to

- estimate and measure with nonstandard units of length (paper clips or string)

- measure lengths in inches and centimeters

- estimate and measure with nonstandard units of volume, weight, and temperature

- tell time to the hour and half hour with digital and analog clocks

- order events by the amount of time they take

- find the date on a calendar

- identify and count money up to $1.00 with pennies, nickels, dimes, and quarters

- estimate amounts by using concrete objects

- make comparisons of length, weight, and volume by using standard and nonstandard units of measure

PROBLEM SOLVING
First graders should be able to

- make and solve word problems by using some of the following strategies:

  – drawing a picture

  – using data from graphs

  – writing a number sentence or equation

  – choosing the operation

  – using a model

- draw reasonable or logical conclusions about situations

- choose the appropriate tool or manipulative to solve a problem

- make connections between different problems

- explain the reasoning used in solving a problem

Pick a Place

Before you begin tutoring, pick a place familiar to the student where he or she feels comfortable. Make sure that you choose a quiet place away from the television, radio, or any other unnecessary distraction. On the other hand, a library might prove too quiet. You want to be able to talk freely with the child. Make sure that a flat surface is available that you can both write on. It doesn't have to be a desk—a kitchen table works just as well.

Set a Time

First select a day and determine the amount of time you would like to spend with the child. Consistency and routine are important for young children. Mornings might work better than afternoons since children are usually more focused early in the day. As you get to know the child, you will become familiar with his or her habits and stamina. Be aware of how long the child can remain focused.

Materials

Make sure that you have the necessary tools to make tutoring a success. Collect pencils, paper, rulers, measuring tools, and scratch paper. Dice, popsicle sticks, or dried beans make excellent manipulatives (hands-on devices) that can be used with the activities in this book. Stickers are a great and inexpensive way to motivate students.

Helpful Hint:
Collect all necessary materials before the session begins. Children will lose interest if the tutor has to search for supplies.

Open the Session

Determine the student's strengths and weaknesses in a given area by giving him or her the pretest provided for each section. His or her performance on the pretest will help you determine where to begin your tutoring practice work. If the student gets only one problem wrong, just go over the problem and move to the next section. The child probably made a simple miscalculation. If a child misses two or three problems, begin by reviewing some of the concepts for that section; if the child misses four or more problems, you may need to introduce (or reteach) the concepts in the section.

Take your cues from the child to determine pacing. It won't happen overnight, but with continued practice and patience, the child will master math!

Introduce New Concepts

When introducing new concepts, provide concrete objects such as beans, toothpicks, or cotton balls for the child to use. These materials will help the child fully understand the concept and prepare him or her for exploring abstract mathematical principles. Encourage the child to talk about the problem while working out the solution. This will enable you to assess his or her understanding of the concept. As much as possible, connect these ideas to the child's world and show him or her how mastering math strategies will be useful.

Questioning

Ask questions that guide the child to discover answers independently. Ask the child to explain how he or she arrived at an answer. If something is not working, try a different approach. Frequently reverse roles and ask the child to pretend that he or she is the tutor. He or she can "teach" you how to do the problems.

Helpful Hint:
Pose open-ended, thought-provoking questions to the student as you help him or her work out math problems.

Practice Makes Perfect

Remember to allow the child enough time to practice and gain confidence in his or her abilities before moving on to the next topic. Give clear directions for each activity. Make sure to wait long enough for the student's answers. Provide extra help when needed. At the close of each session, pick two or three problems for the child to solve. Ask the child to explain how he or she solved them. This book provides a number of practice pages, but they are in no way exhaustive. Use them as a guide to help you create additional problems to assure the student thoroughly understands the concepts.

Helpful Hint:
Watch the child as he or she completes practice items, being alert for any clarification that may be needed. Discuss the process of solving the problems to reinforce the concepts and the strategies.

Ending the Session

If appropriate, give the child an assignment to complete independently before the next session. It is often helpful to have the child explain in advance how he or she will complete the assigned problems.

Before ending the session, make sure that the child has the necessary tools to complete the work. Pencils, paper, a 1–100 number chart, and a box of counting beans will help ensure success. Finally, review the session with the child. Have him or her explain to you the concepts learned and the process or strategies used during the session. Answer any questions the student may have before sending him or her off. End the session on a positive and encouraging note.

Use the following books to help the student develop math skills.

Alexander, Who Used to Be Rich Last Sunday by Judith Viorst (Atheneum, 1985).
A boy spends his only dollar on a variety of irresistible objects.

Anno's Counting Book by Mitsumasa Anno (Harper Collins, 1977).
Children are taken on a journey of their imagination through beautiful landscapes, counting houses, cars, trees, etc.

Caps for Sale: A Tale of a Peddler, Some Monkeys and Their Monkey Business by Esphyr Slobodkina, (Harper Trophy, 1987).
Money and patterning skills are practiced in this tale about a peddler, some monkeys and the trouble they get into.

The Grouchy Ladybug by Eric Carle (Thomas Crowell, 1986).
Children practice time-telling skills as the grouchy ladybug challenges a new animal every hour.

How Big Is a Foot? by Rolf Myller (Atheneum, 1969).
A king runs into trouble with several carpenters as he tries to make a bed for the Queen's birthday present. They all use their feet and come up with different measurements of the queen.

I Know an Old Lady Who Swallowed a Fly by Nadine Wescott (Lothrop, 1989).
A funny tale of a woman who tries to remedy an unusual situation with strange cures. Excellent for learning patterns and sequencing.

Inch by Inch by Leo Lionni (Mulberry Books, 1995).
Follow an inch worm that measures everything in his path and cleverly escapes being eaten by a bird. A great introduction to measurement.

Mouse Count by Ellen Stoll Walsh (Harcourt Brace Jovanovich, 1991).
Follow ten clever mice on a counting adventure as they try to escape being eaten by a snake.

One Hunter by Pat Hutchins (Econo-Clad Books, 1999).
A cute story of a hunter who is watched by the animals as he travels through the forest. Excellent for practicing counting.

Shape Rhymes by Jan Gleiter (Raintree Childrens Books, 1984).
Very cute illustrations and simple poems introduce children to basic two-dimensional shapes.

Use Modeling

It will be helpful to the student if you model some of the strategies that you want to see him or her develop. As you are working through problems together, suggest making a list to organize the data. Would it help to make a chart? Show the child how to draw a picture or make a model that will help him or her solve the problem. Encourage the child to look for and articulate patterns in the problems he or she is working to solve. Suggesting, modeling, and trying out a variety of strategies will help the child develop confidence with these strategies and will increase the likelihood of applying these strategies in the future.

> **Helpful Hint:** Avoid using general praise. Instead try to be specific about praising work or behavior. Use stickers as simple rewards.

Use Real-World Examples

As you work with the child, learn about his or her interests. What are his or her favorite books or movies? Does he enjoy trading cards? Does she like sports? Incorporate these real-world activities into your sessions. Add the scores of a football game. Create a subtraction problem with trading cards.

Manipulatives

Use hands-on materials to keep young minds interested. Collect items such as bottle caps, nature items (sea shells, large seeds), colored wooden beads, buttons, keys, paper clips, and rubber bands. If you travel for tutoring sessions, use plastic zip bags, empty coffee cans, or disposable plastic containers to keep manipulatives organized.

> **Helpful Hint:** Cloth place mats or a table cloth will reduce noise when using manipulatives.

Go Outdoors

Children love to get away from pencil and paper activities and go outside. On the sidewalk, use chalk to draw a number line or hopscotch squares for skip counting. Arrange a life-size pictograph using stuffed animals. Have the student practice measuring capacity by filling cups with sand. Children have wonderful imaginations! Let the child create his or her own math games.

Read a Book

For some sessions, consider using a favorite children's book as a springboard to help explore a mathematical concept from a different perspective. Read the book and discuss the math presented. Write any math problems from the book on a sheet of paper and help the student solve them. Did you get the same answer as the character in the book? Can you think of other problems you can try to solve? See the Literature List on page 8.

Student Survey

1 How much do you like math?

a little   some   a lot

2 How good are you at math?

not very good   OK   very good

3 Would you like to spend more time doing math?

no   maybe   yes

4 How do you like to work on math?

alone   with others   with a friend

5 How often do you use math outside of school?

never   sometimes   all the time

6 Put an **X** next to your favorite subject in school.

Put a ✔ next to your least favorite subject.

____ English   ____ Social Studies

____ Math   ____ Spelling

____ Physical Education   ____ Reading

Note to tutor: A first grader may need assistance reading the questions. Help the child complete the survey, or consider completing the survey orally. Ask the child the questions and discuss his or her responses.

As you work with the student, it is important to help him or her realize that math is not just about memorizing facts. Math is a skill that we use every day and there are many ways to show students the connection between math and our world.

LANGUAGE ARTS

Use Literature

Use literature to explore problem solving with the student. Try beginning with the story *One Hunter* by Pat Hutchins (Econo-Clad Books, 1999) in which the child must figure out how many animals follow the main character in the story. The child will use reading skills and addition to discover how many animals there are at the end of the story.

Make a Book

Help the student make a counting book. Follow the format of a familiar book, such as *Anno's Counting Book* by Mitsumasa Anno (Harper Collins, 1977). First, read the book together and discuss the counting pattern it follows. Then encourage the student to write original sentences and draw pictures to go with the words. Suggest making a counting book about objects in the immediate area. For example: I see one TV; I see two chairs; I see three windows.

Explore Symmetry

Use the alphabet to learn about symmetry. Go through the alphabet and find letters that are symmetrical (that can be divided into two identical parts). Write each letter on a 6" x 6" piece of paper. Make the letter large enough to fill almost the entire page. Ask the student to fold the paper in half. Is the letter the same on both sides? What happens if you fold it the other way?

SCIENCE

Measuring Cups

We frequently need measuring tools for cooking and science experiments. Provide the student with a variety of cups in different sizes. Have the student fill each cup with dried beans or rice. Which cup is closest to a measuring cup? Discuss why we need to use cups to measure things, especially for exact measurements when cooking. Similar comparisons can be made with tablespoons and teaspoons.

Food Fractions

Helpful Hint: Be sure to get parent permission before allowing the child to eat any foods.

Use food to explore fractions with the student. Talk about how to share food, like a sandwich or an orange, between two people. Have the child show you how to divide a pizza or a pie among four people. If possible, use the real object to strengthen the lesson.

ART

Paper Plate Fractions

Paper plates can easily be used to show fractions. Start by folding a plate in half to show two equal parts. Fold the plate again to make fourths. Ask the student to cut out the pieces. Encourage the child to create an animal or an object by using the parts of the plate. The pieces may form a butterfly, a fish, a flower, or anything else. Encourage imagination and creativity!

PHYSICAL EDUCATION

Patterns in Movement

Point out patterns to the student and demonstrate how patterns are part of math. Patterns can be found when we walk, when our hearts beat, and when we move our hands. Be creative and make up movement patterns with the student. Use hands, feet, and props (such as a jump rope) to act out a movement pattern for the student. For example, clap, step, clap, step or hop, hop, stop, hop, hop, stop. Challenge the child to identify the pattern. Take turns creating and identifying patterns.

Math Around the World

A Native American game called Pecan Toss is a fun way to practice and reinforce counting skills. Place whole pecans in a medium-sized plastic bowl. Hold the bowl with two hands and toss the pecans into the air. The object is to try to catch as many nuts in the bowl as possible. Have the student count and record the number of pecans that fall inside and outside of the bowl. Each player takes a turn. The person with the highest number of pecans inside the bowl wins the game. Vary this activity by using more pecans or different shaped bowls.

MATH ALL AROUND US

Money

Money is used everywhere. At the grocery store, encourage the child to read prices, pay for certain items, or use coupons. Did you receive the correct change? At a favorite fast food restaurant, help the

> **Helpful Hint:**
> When working with money, start with play money for counting. Try your local teacher supply or toy store.

child compare two items. Which is less expensive, the hamburger or the cheeseburger?

Geometry

Encourage the child to identify shapes in houses, buildings, or cars. Street signs, such as stop signs, traffic lights, yield signs, and school zone signs will offer a variety of shapes to study. Discuss the meaning of each sign. What does a red octagon tell you to do? (Stop.) Simple maps, such as park or school maps, are also a great way to work with shapes and teach children about landmarks. Discuss how to draw and read a map. Why are maps useful?

Measurement

The study of measurement involves much more than just finding the lengths of objects. We use measurement to compare the size of two objects, to tell time, and to read a calendar. Ask the child to compare his or her height to that of a sibling or other relative. Who is taller or shorter? We use time to know when dinner is served, when our favorite show starts, and how long a movie lasts. Children can read temperature by looking at thermometers posted around the house, at the bank, or at the local pool.

Counting

Counting can be easily practiced as you walk, shop, or drive. The child can count steps, the windows on a building, or the number of red cars he or she sees. Help the child count the number of people waiting in line at the store or the number of stairs he or she has climbed in a parking structure. While you are driving, the child can count the signs or landmarks. Counting is everywhere!

Calendar Fun

A large wall calendar can be used for many activities.

- Point to a date. Ask the child to tell the date in 3 more days; 5 more days.

- Ask the student, "What is your favorite day of the week?" "Why?" Have the student draw a picture of something he or she may do on this day.

- Have the student look at the calendar and skip count by two, five, or ten from the date of a special event (such as a birthday or a vacation).

- Have the student write the ordinal numbers for each day of the month. For example, January 1 is the 1st; January 2 is the 2nd.

Helpful Hint:
Elapsed time is still an abstract idea for first graders. Go slowly.

CONCEPTS FIRST GRADERS SHOULD KNOW

- numbers to 100
- adding and subtracting one- and two-digit numbers to 20
- adding three one-digit numbers
- ordinal numbers from first to tenth
- place value of tens and ones
- comparing and ordering numbers to 100
- inverse operations
- estimation
- simple fractions of a whole (1/2, 1/3, 1/4, 3/4)

ACTIVITIES

Counting Games

Pick a number between 1 and 100. Ask the child to count on from that number and tell you the five numbers that follow. For example, if you choose 23, the student will count 24, 25, and so on. Extend the game and ask the child what number comes before the number you have chosen.

> **Helpful Hint:**
> Incorporate movement or songs into your tutoring sessions. Make it lively and fun!

Once the child is familiar with the concepts of before and after, challenge him or her to figure out 10 more and 10 less than the number. Add some variety to this activity by clapping out the numbers.

Guess My Number

Pick a number between 1 and 100. Have the child try to guess the number. You can only say *higher* or *lower*. The child must keep guessing until he or she gets the right number.

Example:	Guess:	You Say:
21	40	*Lower*
	20	*Higher*
	22	*Lower*
	21	*Correct*

Counting Backwards

Draw a large number line on the ground outside with sidewalk chalk. (Get permission first!) Ask the child to stand on the number 10. Have the child move to

> **Helpful Hint:**
> Vary the types of activities you do with the student. Try to incorporate some of the student's interests into the sessions.

each number on the line as you both count backwards. When you reach 0, say "Blast off!" and the child can pretend to blast into space.

Flash Cards

Purchase or make flash cards for addition and subtraction facts. Write the equation on the front of each card and the answer on the back. As the child practices with these cards, he or she will begin to memorize the facts.

Helpful Hint:
Use stickers as a
reward for good work.

Card Games

Use a deck of playing cards with the face cards removed. The deck is divided evenly between the two players. With the cards facedown, each player takes a turn guessing whether the top card on his or her deck is odd or even. If the player is correct, he or she gets to keep the card. If the player is incorrect, the other player gets the card. The player with the most cards wins.

Domino Addition

Dominos can be used to practice addition and subtraction facts. Place dominos facedown. The child selects a domino, adds the face values of both halves, and writes the equation. Have the student try the same procedure with subtraction. Help the student see the inverse operation ($1 + 2 = 3$ and $3 - 2 = 1$).

100s Collection

Practice counting by making 100s collections with beans, cereal, buttons, or pennies. Place the counted items in resealable plastic bags. Which collection seems bigger? Smaller? If each bag contains 100 items, why does one seem larger than another?

Place Value

Wooden craft sticks with beans glued to them are an excellent way to practice counting place value. Each bean on the stick represents a one. Once there are 10 beans on a stick, it becomes a ten. (These are also great for practice counting by tens.) Glue ten beans onto a craft stick. Lay the stick vertically in the tens column on a place value chart. Place five beans in the ones column. Ask the student to tell you the value in each column. How many are in the tens column? In the ones column? What number does that make? Practice the same way, using a variety of numbers.

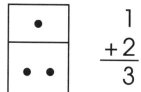

tens	ones

Lima Beans

Spray paint lima beans with a bright color on one side. Give the child a cup with five lima beans in it. Shake the cup and dump out the beans. Ask the child to create an equation, using beans with one color side up as one number and with the other color side up as another. For example: 3 red, 2 white is $3 + 2 = 5$. Extend this activity by including more beans or asking the child to create a simple word problem.

Dice Numbers

Roll two dice and have the child create the largest possible two-digit number with those two numbers. Record the student's number. Then have him or her create the smallest possible two-digit number with the same two numbers, and record it. For example, if the child rolls 3 and 6, the largest number would be 63, and the smallest would be 36. Vary this activity by adding or subtracting the digits.

Clap Counting

Pick a number between 1 and 100. Clap a few times and ask the child to count along and tell you which number you end on. For example, start with 56 and clap twice; the child should respond with 58.

Ordinal Numbers

The student can practice ordinal numbers by drawing a simple picture of his or her family and friends. Help the child label each person in the picture with ordinal numbers. Who is the first person in the picture? The fourth? For variety, try arranging a number of objects in a line on the table. Pose questions that require the student to use ordinal numbers.

Making Comparisons

Research the length of several dinosaurs from tail to snout. Which dinosaur was the longest? The shortest? Remind the child that when comparing two numbers, he or she should always start with the digit in the highest place value (at the left). If the digits are the same, move to the next digit (to the right) and compare the numbers the same way. With practice, this skill becomes second nature for children and helps them prepare for working with larger numbers.

which is longer?

All in Order

Use an almanac to locate the heights of several famous buildings in your state. Help the student analyze the information and arrange the buildings from tallest to shortest. For variety, have the student find the cost of four favorite toys for the year. Which is the cheapest? Most expensive? Help the student arrange the costs in order from least to most expensive. What is the difference between the least and most expensive?

How tall is it?

Oceans of Numbers

Count how many.

1

2

_____   _____

Solve. Watch the signs.

3 🐟🐟 + 🐟🐟🐟 =

4 🐟🐟🐟🐟🐟 – 🐟🐟 =

5   8
     +7

6   12
     – 10

7   3
      5
     +2

Fill in the missing numbers.

8 2, 4, ____, 8, 10, ____, ____

9 5, 10, ____, 20, ____, ____

11
tens	ones
2	6

What is the number?

_____

 Name

Nuts about Numbers

Count how many nuts are in each group.

1

2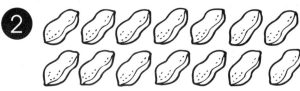

_____   _____

Fill in the missing numbers.

3

4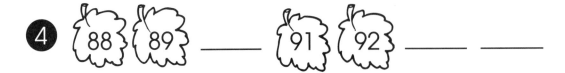

Write how many tens and ones. Then write the number.

5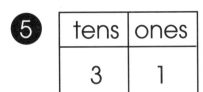

6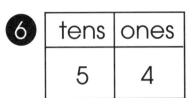

___ tens ___ ones = _____   ___ tens ___ ones = _____

FS122129 The Tutor's Handbook: Math Grade 1

 Name

Magical Numbers

Add. Check your work, using subtraction.

1
$$\begin{array}{r} 1 \\ +2 \\ \hline 3 \end{array} \qquad \begin{array}{r} 3 \\ -2 \\ \hline 1 \end{array}$$

2
$$\begin{array}{r} 7 \\ +4 \\ \hline \end{array}$$

3
$$\begin{array}{r} 9 \\ +9 \\ \hline \end{array}$$

Subtract. Check your work, using addition.

4
$$\begin{array}{r} 2 \\ -1 \\ \hline 1 \end{array} \qquad \begin{array}{r} 1 \\ +1 \\ \hline 2 \end{array}$$

5
$$\begin{array}{r} 5 \\ -3 \\ \hline \end{array}$$

6
$$\begin{array}{r} 8 \\ -5 \\ \hline \end{array}$$

Use > or <.

7 12 _____ 20

8 81 _____ 48

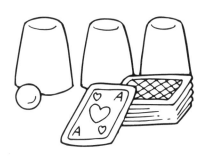

FS122129 The Tutor's Handbook: Math Grade 1

 Name

Beach Day

1 Color the fourth beach ball.

2 Color the tenth shovel.

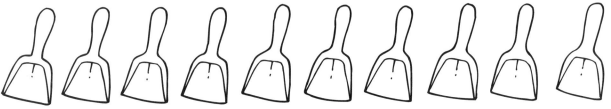

3 Color the sixth sea star.

4 Color the correct amount for each circle.

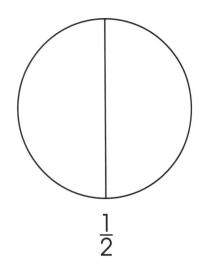 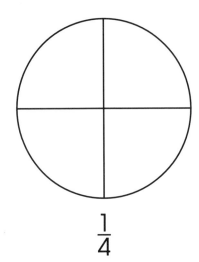 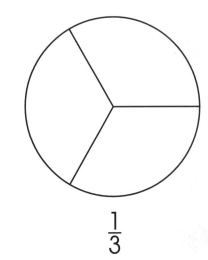

$\frac{1}{2}$ $\qquad$ $\frac{1}{4}$ $\qquad$ $\frac{1}{3}$

FS122129 The Tutor's Handbook: Math Grade 1

Juggling Numbers

Count how many.

 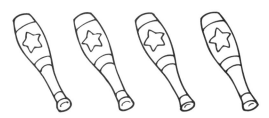

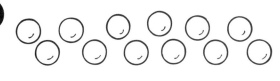

_____   _____

Add or subtract.

3 $6 + 8 =$ _____

4 $7 + 4 =$ _____

5 $8 - 3 =$ _____

6 $10 - 7 =$ _____

7
$$\begin{array}{r} 12 \\ +\ 9 \\ \hline \end{array}$$

8
$$\begin{array}{r} 16 \\ +\ 3 \\ \hline \end{array}$$

9
$$\begin{array}{r} 17 \\ -\ 4 \\ \hline \end{array}$$

10
$$\begin{array}{r} 15 \\ -\ 3 \\ \hline \end{array}$$

Use > or <.

11   37 _____ 41

12   60 _____ 50

CONCEPTS FIRST GRADERS SHOULD KNOW

- identifying, predicting, and extending shape and number patterns
- comparing numbers by using *between*, *before*, and *after*
- skip counting to 100 by 2, 5, and 10
- fact families for addition and subtraction

Helpful Hint:
Ask the following questions:
What makes this a pattern?
How would you describe the pattern?
What is the next step in the pattern?

ACTIVITIES

Building Walls

Have the student use pattern blocks (found at teacher supply or toy stores) to build an imaginary wall. The wall should be a continuous pattern with no open spaces. The child must use his or her skills to predict and extend the pattern. Have the child describe his or her pattern to you, explaining what shapes were used.

Pattern Game

Begin the game with lots of geometric shapes cut out of construction paper. The first player will create a pattern by using three or four of the shapes. He or she asks, "What shape goes next?" The opponent must select the correct shape to complete the pattern. If the guess is correct, the second player scores a point and gets to make the next pattern. If the guess is incorrect, the other person scores a point and gets to continue. Start with simple patterns and get more complex as the student's understanding of patterns improves.

Pattern Trains

By using linking cubes or colored blocks, the student can create his or her own "trains" to practice patterning. Trains can be simple or complex; the child can keep adding more and more "cars" to the train. This activity encourages the student to use his or her imagination, practice extending patterns, and have fun all at the same time!

Jewelry Patterns

The student can use beads, noodles, or cereal to make bracelets or necklaces. Give the child a piece of string with a knot at one end. Encourage the child to create a pattern. For variety, noodles and cereal can be painted or dyed. Try using beads of various sizes and textures.

Partner Patterns

Sit across from the student. Place a divider between you and the student so that you cannot see one another's patterns. Build a simple shape pattern with pattern blocks. Without showing the student, verbally describe how to build the pattern. For example, "Start with a red octagon and put green triangles on each side." Continue with the directions until the student completes the shape pattern on his or her side of the divider. Take away the divider and compare the two patterns. The child should see two identical shape patterns. Once the child is comfortable with this, reverse roles. Have the student build a pattern and give you instructions on how to build it.

> **Helpful Hint:**
> Counting objects by numbers other than one can be accomplished much more quickly than counting one object at a time. Finding and using counting patterns will make solving difficult problems easier.

Counting Tape

Start with a long strip of calculator tape. Have the child draw vertical lines to create squares and then fill in the squares with the numbers 1 to 20.

1	2	3	4	5	6	7	8	9	10

Have the student show odd numbers by coloring every other box. The even numbered boxes will be uncolored. The child can use the pattern to help remember odd and even numbers and practice counting. He or she can add on to the counting tape by writing in more numbers all the way up to 100. Extend this activity to practice skip counting by 2, 5, and 10.

100s number patterns

Begin with a 1–100 number chart. Have the student color every other number, beginning with 2. Demonstrate that these colored numbers make a pattern and show how to count by 2. Explain that coloring every tenth space, beginning with 1, shows a different pattern and reveals how to count by 10. Once the child can count by 2, 5, and 10, omit some of the numbers on the chart and have the student fill in the missing numbers.

Helpful Hint: Using counters (dried beans or popcorn seeds) to cover the numbers on the number chart enables the child to look for patterns and use the chart again and again.

Fact Families

Fact families are addition and subtraction or multiplication and division facts that use the same numbers. There are four facts in each fact family. Write out a math problem that the child knows, such as $3 + 4 = 7$. Help the child see that he or she also knows that $4 + 3 = 7$, $7 - 4 = 3$, and $7 - 3 = 4$. Give the child the numbers for a fact family and ask him or her to write all of the facts. Practice with this helps the child memorize basic math facts.

High Five

To help the student practice counting by 5, give him or her "high fives." Each time you touch the student's hand, count by 5. Count up to 100. The same practice can be done counting by 10, but this time use both hands. Counting will become easier the more the student practices.

1-100 Number Chart

1	2	3	4	5	6	7	8	9	10
11	12	13	14	15	16	17	18	19	20
21	22	23	24	25	26	27	28	29	30
31	32	33	34	35	36	37	38	39	40
41	42	43	44	45	46	47	48	49	50
51	52	53	54	55	56	57	58	59	60
61	62	63	64	65	66	67	68	69	70
71	72	73	74	75	76	77	78	79	80
81	82	83	84	85	86	87	88	89	90
91	92	93	94	95	96	97	98	99	100

Name

Ship Shape

Finish the shape pattern.

1   _____ _____ _____

2   _____ _____ _____

Finish the pattern.

3

3	4	5	3	4				

4

A	A	B	A	A				

Fill in the missing numbers

5 4 _____ 8 _____ 12

6 15 20 25 _____ _____ 40

7 Write a fact family for 2, 3, 5.

2 + 3 = 5	

25
reproducible

FS122129 The Tutor's Handbook: Math Grade 1

 Name

Ship Mates

Follow the pattern to find the next shape. For example:

Finish the pattern.

1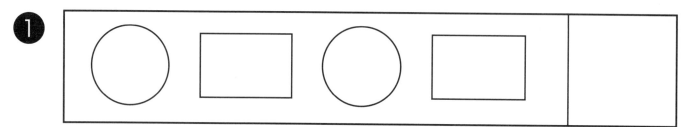

2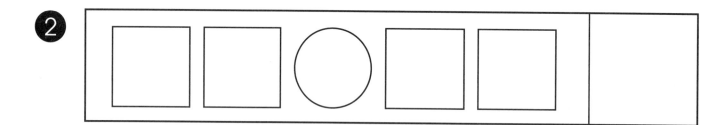

3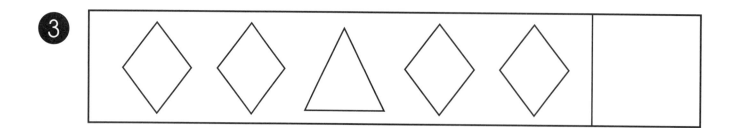

4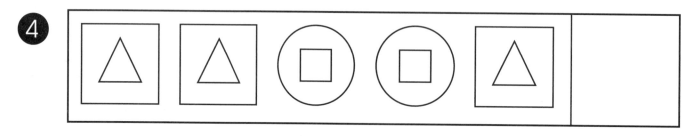

FS122129 The Tutor's Handbook: Math Grade 1

 Name

Puppy Love

Follow the pattern. Show what comes next.

1

| 2 | 3 | 4 | 2 | 3 | 4 | 2 | | |

2

| 3 | 3 | 4 | 4 | 3 | 3 | 4 | | |

Count by 2, 5, or 10 to complete the patterns.

3

4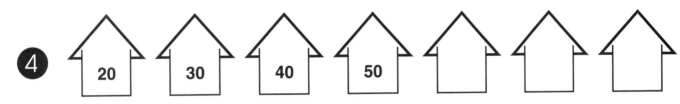

5 5, 10, 15, ____, 25, ____

6 65, 70, ____, ____, ____, 90

FS122129 The Tutor's Handbook: Math Grade 1

Family Fun

If you know that 3 + 4 = 7,
then you also know that
4 + 3 = 7, 7 – 3 = 4, and 7 – 4 = 3.

Write a fact family in each box.

①

3	1	4

3 + 1 = 4

②

7	8	15

③

6	5	11

④

4	9	13

FS122129 The Tutor's Handbook: Math Grade 1

Name

Pattern Finale

Finish the shape pattern.

1   ____ ____

2    ____ ____

Finish the pattern.

3

7	8	9	7	8	9			

4

A	B	B	A	B	B			

Fill in the missing numbers.

5 35 _____ 55 _____ _____

6 70 _____ 90 100 _____

7 Complete the fact family for 4, 5, 9.

4 + 5 = 9	

FS122129 The Tutor's Handbook: Math Grade 1

CONCEPTS FIRST GRADERS SHOULD KNOW

- two-dimensional shapes—square, triangle, rectangle, and circle
- three-dimensional objects—sphere, cylinder, cone, and pyramid
- lines of symmetry
- relationship of objects in space (near, far, above, below)

ACTIVITIES

Sorting Shapes

Give the student a variety of wooden blocks. Help the child become familiar with the blocks by showing him or her the number of corners, the number of sides, and the size of each block. Ask the child to make up a rule for sorting the shapes. For example: shapes with corners and shapes without corners. Encourage the child to apply various rules.

Building Blocks

Have the student use the wooden blocks to build something. Encourage imagination and creativity! Ask the student to name and describe the shapes he or she uses. Review counting skills by asking him or her to count how many of each shape is used in the building.

Geometry Hunt

Go on a Geometry Hunt around the building, or playground, or in the neighborhood. Help the child search for geometric structures and shapes. Help the student look for buildings in the shapes of cubes or for rectangular windows and doors. Have the student find the cylindrical shape of a telephone pole. Explain that some shapes may be hidden and encourage the child to practice looking with a "geometric eye." Have the child record the objects on a shapes chart.

Helpful Hint:
It is important for the student to learn and use correct geometric vocabulary. Model and encourage correct usage when manipulating objects or problem solving.

Inventions

Supply the child with a variety of paper or cardboard shapes, such as toilet paper rolls, tissue boxes, shoe boxes, and oatmeal canisters. Ask the child what he or she would build with the given materials. If the child has trouble getting started, ask him or her how he or she would improve on an existing invention, such as a car, a robot, or a bicycle. Allow the child time to construct the invention and then ask him or her to take you on a tour of the device, explaining all of its components. Remind the student to use the geometric names for the shapes or objects.

Tracing

Start by having the student trace simple two-dimensional shapes, such as circles, triangles, and squares. Then provide the child with a cylinder, a cube, and a prism. Ask the child what would happen if he or she traced the face of a cylinder (circle) or the face of a cube (square). Allow the student time to trace the faces of these three-dimensional shapes. Discuss the results.

Shape Monsters

Ask the child to draw a shape such as a circle, triangle, or rectangle. Then have him or her create a shape monster by adding arms, legs, and facial features. Ask the student to give the monster a name such as Timmy Triangle or Sally Square. This activity takes no time at all, and the kids love it!

Timmy Triangle

Shape Pictures

Provide lots of pieces of construction paper that have been cut into various geometric shapes such as triangles, squares, rectangles, and circles. Ask the child to arrange the shapes in a design. If the child has trouble getting started, you might suggest a train, a barn, a Ferris wheel, or an animal. Encourage the child to use his or her imagination when designing. While he or she is gluing the shapes onto a large piece of plain paper, ask the child to identify the shapes and explain how they work together. Why did you use these shapes to design an elephant? What about the triangle reminded you of a fish?

Symmetry

Draw a variety of shapes. Ask the student to draw the line of symmetry through each shape. Make sure that the student knows that when a shape is symmetrical, both parts are the same size and shape. As an extension, the student can create his or her own symmetrical objects on paper. Have the student fold a piece of paper in half lengthwise and then draw a shape on the front, starting at the fold (see illustration). Let the child cut out the shape and unfold it. The fold in the paper shows the line of symmetry.

Cartoon Characters

Have the child create a cartoon character (Super Geo!) designed only with geometric shapes. Encourage the child to use his or her imagination when creating the character. Remind the student that only formal geometric shapes, such as circles, squares, triangles, and rectangles, may be used. It may be necessary to show the child how the same shape can appear different when various lengths are used. For example, a rectangle can be wide or narrow. Connect this activity to language arts by helping the child create a story for the cartoon character.

Flash Cards

Use magazines or old books to find pictures of different objects that have distinctive shapes (a basketball, table, or tire). Make sure the image is easily recognizable. Glue each picture to the front of a 3" x 5" note card. Write the name of each shape on the back. Use the flash cards to help the student practice recognizing and naming shapes.

Dots

By using a dot grid, the student can practice making various geometric shapes. Prepare a one-page dot grid and make multiple photocopies. Show the student how to connect the dots to make squares, triangles, and other geometric shapes. To prepare for measuring area, he or she can count the number of dots used to make the shapes.

> **Helpful Hint:**
> Use geoboards (available at your local teacher supply store) and rubber bands when practicing geometric shapes.

Geometric Fractions

Supply paper cutouts of several shapes, such as circles, rectangles, or hexagons. Have the student fold or draw and cut along the line of symmetry. Help him or her see how the pieces represent fractions. A hexagon divided in half creates 2 trapezoids. If divided into sixths, the hexagon becomes 6 triangles. As the shapes are divided into fractions, they create other shapes. What shapes can you find if a square is divided in half? What fractions do you need to create 2 squares from a rectangle?

Shape Up

1 How many sides? _____

2 How many sides? _____

3 How many vertices? _____

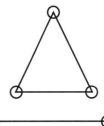

4 How many vertices? _____

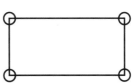

Match the name with each figure.

5 triangle

6 cone

7 square

8 cube

a.

b.

c.

d.

Match It

Copy each shape.

1 rectangle

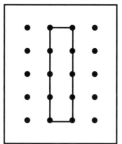 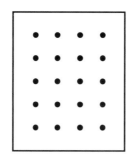

2 square

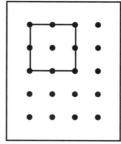 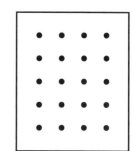

3 triangle

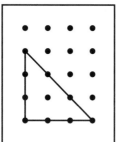 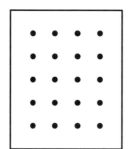

4 hexagon

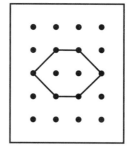 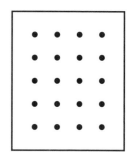

5 octagon

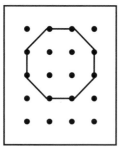 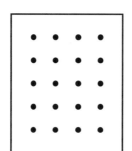

6 rectangle

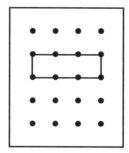 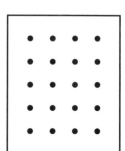

7 pentagon

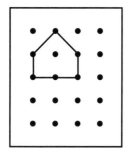 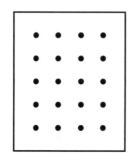

8 triangle

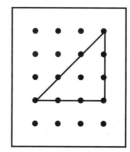 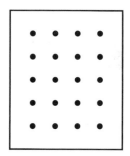

FS122129 The Tutor's Handbook: Math Grade 1

 Name

Similar Solids

Put an X on the object that does not belong.

 1

| sphere |      |

 2

| cone |      |

 3

| cube | 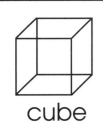     |

 4

| cylinder |      |

 5

| rectangular prism | 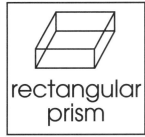     |

FS122129 The Tutor's Handbook: Math Grade 1

 **Name**

How Many?

How many sides?

 1

___4___ sides

2
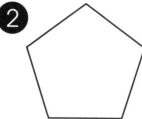

_____ sides

3

_____ sides

4

_____ sides

How many vertices?

5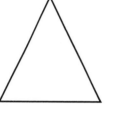

___5___ vertices

6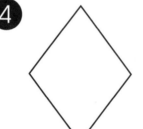

_____ vertices

7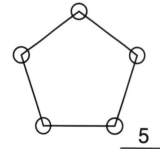

_____ vertices

8

_____ vertices

FS122129 The Tutor's Handbook: Math Grade 1

 Name

Go for Geometry

Circle the correct name for each shape.

1

square   rectangle

2
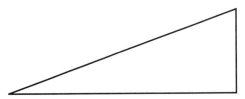

triangle   oval

3

cone   cylinder

4

cube   pyramid

5 How many sides? _____

6 How many vertices? _____

Put an X on the shape that does not belong.

7

 sphere

FS122129 The Tutor's Handbook: Math Grade 1

CONCEPTS FIRST GRADERS SHOULD KNOW

- estimating and measuring by using nonstandard units of length, volume, weight, and temperature
- lengths in inches and centimeters
- time to the hour and half hour on digital and analog clocks
- ordering events by the amount of time they take
- using a calendar
- counting money to $1.00 with pennies, nickels, dimes, and quarters
- estimating amounts by using concrete objects
- comparing lengths, weights, volumes, and temperatures

ACTIVITIES

Comparing Sizes

Start discussing measurement in terms of size comparisons (taller or shorter, bigger or smaller, higher or lower). Keep it simple and use objects that are familiar to the child. For example, provide two toys and ask "Which toy is larger?"

Helpful Hint:

Begin measurement with nonstandard units of measure such as paper clip lengths. Once the child has mastered these, move on to standard units of measure.

String Measurement

A piece of string can serve as a nonstandard unit of measurement. Give the child a piece of string of any length. Have him or her find something that is shorter than the string and then draw a picture to record the item. Ask the child to find something that is longer and something that is the same length as the piece of string. Remind him or her to record the findings, then compare.

Teddy Bear Measurement

Ask the child to measure his or her favorite stuffed animal. Begin by asking the child to estimate how big the animal's head is and to cut a piece of yarn of that length. Tape the piece of yarn on a paper and label it *guess*. Give the child a tape measure to measure around the animal's head. Help him or her cut a piece of yarn to that length and tape it to the paper. Label it *actual*. Compare the actual measurement with the length of the guess yarn. Talk about the difference and how close the guess was to the actual measurement. For an extension, have the child estimate the length of his or her own hands, arms, or feet and measure the same way.

Hand and Foot Ruler

Hands can be used as another nonstandard unit of measure. Have the student put a hand on the table and show him or her how to measure with a hand length from small finger to thumb. Show the student how to mark the point and then measure with the other hand, counting all the way across the table. Measuring can also be done with a foot. Ask the child to estimate the length of the room in which he or she is working. Then have him or her measure, counting steps heel-to-toe to get the correct amount.

Calendar

Provide a calendar. A large, twelve-month wall calendar works well. Explain to the student how the year is divided into 12 months, 52 weeks, 365 days, and 4 seasons. Draw outlines around each season or fill in days with seasonal symbols (orange leaves for fall, snowflakes for winter). Discuss elapsed time. Ask the child to count the number of days until the weekend. Let the child record events such as birthdays, holidays, or other expected activities. How long has it been since winter break? Since summer break? How many more weeks until your birthday?

Spending Money

> **Helpful Hint:** Using real coins helps young children recognize and understand the value of money.

Give the child a specific money amount. Help him or her learn to count up or down from that amount. For example: starting with 30 cents, have him or her count up to 43 cents. Show the student a dime and three pennies. Help him or her count 30, plus 10 is forty, forty-one, forty-two, forty-three. Extend this activity by playing store with the child. He or she can "purchase" items such as stickers or treats from your "store."

Volume

Bring in juice or milk cartons of various sizes. Use these to introduce the concept of volume. Compare the amounts of liquid in a gallon, half gallon, quart, and pint. First, ask the student to estimate the number of quarts or pints it would take to fill up a half-gallon container. Record the student's guess and then help him or her do actual measuring. Encourage the student to record the number of pints or quarts it takes to fill the half gallon. Ask him or her to compare the actual measurement with the estimate. Repeat the same procedure for a gallon. Help the student discover the relationship between quarts, pints, and gallons.

Weight

Help the child weigh him- or herself in both pounds and kilograms on a bathroom scale. Record the results. Ask the child to find an object that he or she estimates weighs more and an object that weighs less than him- or herself. Record the estimated weights. If possible, weigh the objects. Discuss why some things weigh more or less than others. Explain that a solid object, such as a child, will weigh more than a hollow object, such as a vase, even if both are about the same size.

Metric	U.S. Customary
length 1 centimeter = 10 millimeters 1 decimeter = 10 centimeters 1 meter = 10 decimeters **mass/weight** 1 kilogram = 1,000 grams **capacity** 1 liter = 1,000 milliliters	**length** 1 foot = 12 inches 1 yard = 3 feet 1 mile = 5,280 feet **mass/weight** 1 pound = 16 ounces 1 ton = 2,000 pounds **capacity** 1 cup = 8 fluid ounces 1 pint = 2 cups 1 quart = 2 pints 1 gallon = 4 quarts

Standard Measurement

Give the student a ruler, yard stick, or measuring tape and help him or her measure various items. Make it fun by asking the child to find specific lengths. For example: ask the student to find something that is 10 inches long. Finding objects that are in a given size range will provide practice with estimation and measuring skills.

> **Helpful Hint:** Some first graders are inexperienced with using standard measurement tools. Some students may need assistance learning how to read inch or centimeter rulers.

Time

Make a clock, using a paper plate for the face. Help the child write the numbers as they appear on a wall clock. Use 2 different-color pieces of sturdy construction paper for the hands. Cut a long hand (minutes) and a short hand (hour). Attach both hands to the center of the face with a brass fastener. Help the child practice telling time by using the clock he or she made! Write times that need practice on note cards so that the child can practice individually.

Recipes

Prepare a simple recipe, such as instant pudding. (Make sure to get a parent's permission.) Have the child read the directions on the package (help with reading as necessary). Help the student measure the amount of dried pudding mix. How many cups? Help the child pour the milk as called for by the directions. Prepare the pudding as directed. Enjoy the tasty treat!

Measurement Fun

Color the longer object green.

Color the shorter object purple.

 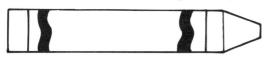   

Write the number of units.

 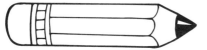   

_____ inches   _____ centimeters

Write the time.

    _____ : _____    _____ : _____

How much money is shown?

                                        _____ ¢

                                        _____ ¢

FS122129 The Tutor's Handbook: Math Grade 1

 Name

Measurement and Money

Use a ruler to find the units.

____ cm

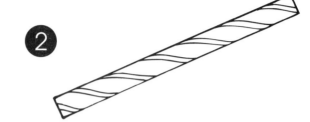

____ cm

 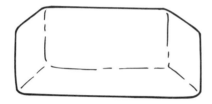

____ in.

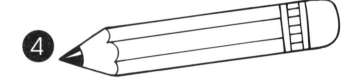

____ in.

Count the money.

penny	nickel	dime	quarter

____ ¢

____ ¢

FS122129 The Tutor's Handbook: Math Grade 1

Name

Gobble, Gobble

November						
Sun	Mon	Tues	Wed	Thurs	Fri	Sat
		1	2	3	4	5
6	7	8	9	10	11	12
13	14	15	16	17	18	19
20	21	22	23	24 Thanksgiving	25	26
27	28	29	30			

1. What is the name of this month? _____

2. How many days are in this month? _____

3. What day of the week is the 5th? _____

4. What is the date for Thanksgiving? _____

5. How many Tuesdays are in there in this month? _____

Time for Fun

What time is it?

_____:_____

2

_____:_____

_____:_____

Match the clocks.

4 | **1:00**   a.

5 | **10:30**   b.

6 | **5:00**   c.

7 | **7:30**   d.

FS122129 The Tutor's Handbook: Math Grade 1

Measure Up

Color the longest pencil.

1
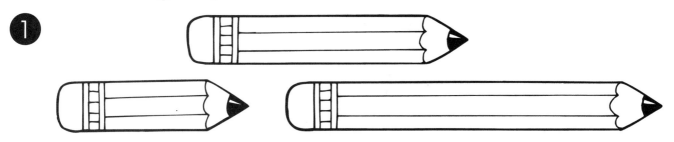

Use a ruler to find the number of units.

2

3

_____ in.   _____ cm

Write the time.

4

_____:_____

Write the money amount.

5

_____ ¢

CONCEPTS FIRST GRADERS SHOULD KNOW

- using tables, patterns, and sequence to explore relationships
- the terms *more*, *less*, and *as many as*
- number sets to 100
- collecting, organizing, displaying, and comparing data in simple graphs and tables with concrete objects, pictures, or numbers

ACTIVITIES

Fruit Sort

Provide the student with a variety of fruit—apples (green and red), bananas, pears, oranges, lemons, limes, strawberries, blackberries, and so on. Encourage the child to determine how to sort the fruit into groups. Will you sort by color? Texture? Type of fruit? Ask the child to arrange the fruit groups in horizontal rows. Use a large piece of paper to label each group. The student has just made a bar graph with real objects!

Helpful Hint: Vary the orientation of graphs. Present some graphs vertically and some horizontally.

Weather Graph

Ask the student to record the weather for 1 week (parents can help). Divide a large piece of construction paper into 4 parts. Use simple pictures to represent sunny, rainy, cloudy, and windy conditions. Provide the child with at least 7 clothespins. Explain to the student that each day he or she should attach a clothespin to the square that shows what the weather was like on that day. Remind the child to bring the record to the next tutoring session. Help the child make a graph to show the weather for that week.

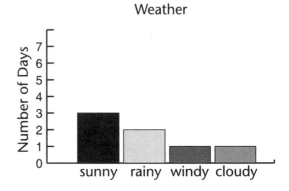

Weather

Survey Time

Have the child take a survey of his or her friends and family. Give the student a T-chart on which to record answers. On the left of the T-chart, head the column *Favorite Color*. List several colors that people might choose as a favorite—blue, red, green, yellow, purple, or orange. On the right of the T-chart, head the column *Responses*. Show the child how to record by using tally marks. Remind him or her to use a crosshatch as the fifth tally.

Favorite Color	Responses
Green	卌 II
Blue	III
Red	卌

At the following session, discuss the results with the child. Which color was the most popular? How many more people liked green than blue? Extend this activity by helping the child to create a bar graph showing the results of the survey. On other occasions, encourage the student to use other subjects for a survey, such as favorite sports, favorite TV shows, or favorite foods.

> **Helpful Hint:**
> **Probability is the prediction or analysis of the likelihood that a certain event will occur. Something is equally likely to happen if all of the possible outcomes have the same chance of occurring.**

Dice

Have the child roll a single die 20 times and use tally marks to record how many times a certain number is rolled.

Example:

Which number did you roll the most?

The least?

Are you more or less likely to roll a particular number?

Flip a Coin

Ask the child to flip a coin 10 times and record the results. After 10 flips, ask the child to predict what will come next. Help the child realize that there is a 50 percent chance for either heads or tails. Why is there a 50/50 chance?

Heads	⊥⊥⊤ I
Tails	IIII

Checkers Grab Bag

Put 10 red checkers and 5 black checkers in a small paper bag. Ask the child to guess which color he or she will probably get when a checker is drawn from the bag. Have the child take a checker from the bag. Was it the same as the guess? Repeat this activity several times. How many times did the child guess correctly? Why were more red checkers drawn than black checkers?

Spinners

Another way to reinforce probability concepts is to use a spinner. Using a marker, divide a paper plate or cardboard circle into fourths. Color three fourths of the plate purple. Color one fourth of the plate green. As you are coloring the circle, introduce fractions by explaining and naming the fraction you are creating. In the center attach a pointer made from posterboard or card stock. Use a brass fastener to attach the pointer. Ask the child to predict how many times the spinner will land on purple or green and to record the results. Pose questions that require the child to provide reasoning for the prediction. Spin the hand 12 times. How many times did the spinner land on purple? On green? Were the child's predictions correct?

purple	⊥⊥⊤ IIII
green	III

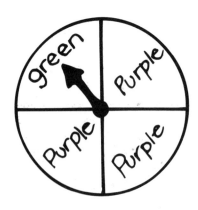

Name

Reading a Graph

Shapes

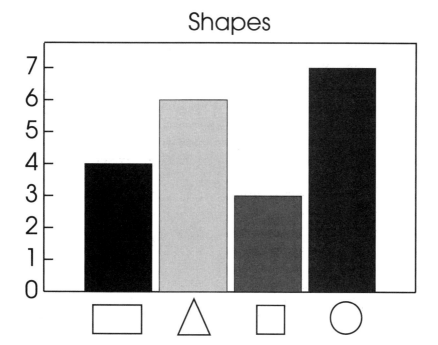

1. How many ▭ ? _____

2. How many △ ? _____

3. How many ☐ ? _____

4. How many ○ ? _____

5. Which has the most? _____

6. Which has the least? _____

7. How many more ○ than ▭ ? _____

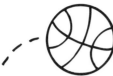 # Recess Time

Favorite Recess Activity

kickball	IIII
basketball	JHT IIII
hopscotch	II
jungle gym	III
tetherball	JHT II

Fill in the bar graph.

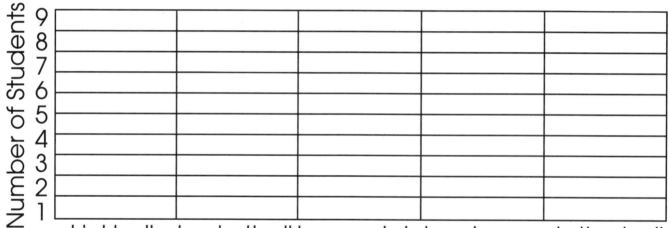

Number of Students

kickball   basketball   hopscotch   jungle gym   tetherball

Activities

1 Which game did most people choose? _____

2 How many more people chose kickball than hopscotch? _____

FS122129 The Tutor's Handbook: Math Grade 1

 Name

Probably Paula

1 In this bag there are 12 blue marbles and 4 purple marbles. If Paula were to reach into the bag and pull out a marble, what color would she most likely pull out?

_____

Look at the spinner.

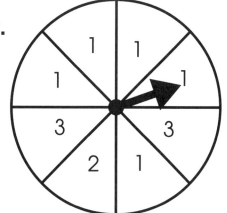

2 How many 1s are on the spinner? _____

How many 2s are on the spinner? _____

How many 3s are on the spinner? _____

3 Which number is Paula most likely to spin? _____

4 Which number is Paula least likely to spin? _____

FS122129 The Tutor's Handbook: Math Grade 1

 Name _____

Cars

Uncle Joe's Car-O-Rama sells lots of cars each month. Look at the bar graph and answer the questions below.

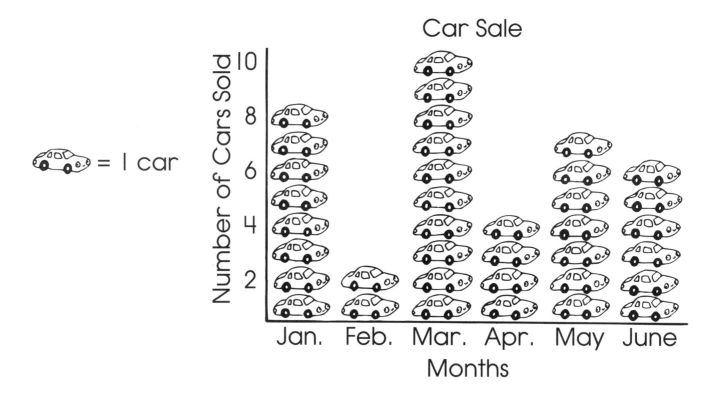

① How many cars were sold in January? _____

② How many cars were sold in May? _____

③ In which month were the most cars sold? _____

④ In which month were the fewest cars sold? _____

⑤ How many more cars were sold in April than in

February? _____

FS122129 The Tutor's Handbook: Math Grade 1

 Name

Perfect Pets

Favorite Pets

frogs	ll
dogs	llll l
cats	lll
birds	l

Favorite Pets

frogs				
dogs				
cats				
birds				

1 Which pet did children like the most? _____

2 Which pet did children like the least? _____

3 How many more children chose a dog than

a bird? _____

Look at the spinner.

4 Which number are you most

likely to spin? _____

5 Which number are you least

likely to spin? _____

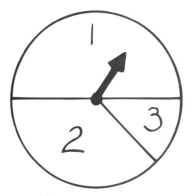

FS122129 The Tutor's Handbook: Math Grade 1

It is important to help the child understand that he or she is developing a variety of strategies that will help him or her solve math problems. A strategy is simply a plan that may be used to solve a problem. Choosing an appropriate strategy is the challenge. A sufficient understanding of the different strategies the child has mastered will enable him or her to think the problem through and select the best one to use to solve a particular problem.

> **Helpful Hint:**
> **Be sensitive to the child's reading level. Let the child do the math, but help him or her with the reading.**

If the child is unsuccessful in solving a problem, help him or her with an alternative approach to the problem. Talking through a number of different problems helps the child develop more sophisticated problem-solving skills. In fact, the process that the student goes through to solve the problem is as important as the correct solution.

As you help the student solve a variety of problems, encourage him or her to recall some of the strategies he or she has developed.

Can you make a table or graph with the information?

Would it help you to draw a picture?

What is the problem asking you to do?

Which operation should you use (addition, subtraction)?

What are the key words in the problem that help you know what to do (altogether, in all, more than, less than, take away)?

Can you find a pattern?

Can you make a guess and test the answer?

As you work with the child, remember the benefit of having him or her talk about his or her thinking process. Respond and ask additional questions that will help the child discover that there is often more than one way to solve a given problem. Help the child evaluate these possibilities and determine the best course of action.

Remind children of the steps necessary to solve a problem.

- **think**   What is the problem asking?
- **search**   What facts does the problem give? How will I solve it?
- **solve**   Compute the answer—this may require more than one step.
- **check**   Does my answer make sense? Does it answer the question?

Consider listing these steps on a chart and continually review them until they become automatic.

Toy Problems

Solve.

1 _____ + 6 = 14

2 3 + _____ = 20

Solve the word problems.

3 Mindy had 5 dolls. She lost 2 of them. How many dolls does she have left?

_____ dolls

4 Dan got 3 yo-yos for his birthday. He bought 4 more. How many does he have in all?

_____ yo-yos

5 There were 10 apples in the basket. Four more were on the floor. How many apples were there altogether?

_____ apples

6 Sandy went to the beach. She collected 20 sea shells. She dropped 5 of them. How many does she have now?

_____ sea shells

FS122129 The Tutor's Handbook: Math Grade 1

 Name

Tricky Problems

Use subtraction to find each missing number.

1 $5 + \underline{3} = 8$ $\qquad$ $\begin{array}{r} 8 \\ -\ 5 \\ \hline 3 \end{array}$ $\qquad$ **2** $4 + \underline{} = 10$

3 $11 + \underline{} = 15$ $\qquad\qquad\qquad$ **4** $\underline{} + 3 = 9$

Use addition to find each missing number.

5 $\underline{7} - 2 = 5$ $\qquad$ $\begin{array}{r} 5 \\ +\ 2 \\ \hline 7 \end{array}$ $\qquad$ **6** $\underline{} - 8 = 12$

7 $\underline{} - 6 = 4$ $\qquad\qquad\qquad$ **8** $\underline{} - 10 = 8$

Fill in the missing number.

9 $3 + \underline{} = 6 + 3$ $\qquad\qquad$ **10** $\underline{} + 4 = 4 + 2$

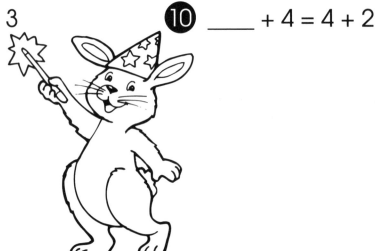

FS122129 The Tutor's Handbook: Math Grade 1

Friendship

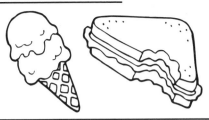

Solve the following word problems.

1 Tran had 3 snakes. She found 2 more in the garden. How many snakes does she have altogether?

_____ snakes

2 Milo bought 6 packs of gum. He gave 2 packs to his friend. How many packs does Milo have left?

_____ packs

3 Tom had 4 trading cards. He bought 3 more on Saturday. How many cards does he have in total?

_____ cards

4 Sarah spent $2.00 for an ice cream and $3.00 for a soda. What is the sum of the money she spent?

_____ dollars

5 There are 10 sandwiches on the table. Three of them were eaten. How many sandwiches are left?

_____ sandwiches

6 There were 7 children playing at the park. Two more children arrived. How many children are there altogether?

_____ children

FS122129 The Tutor's Handbook: Math Grade 1

 Name

Story Problems

Solve the following word problems.

---

1 Pat made 6 greeting cards. She gave 3 away. How many cards are left?

_____ cards

---

2 There are 5 children playing tag. Two more children join the game. How many children are playing?

_____ children

---

3 Mario has 7 flowers in his garden. Barbara has 4 flowers. How many more flowers does Mario have than Barbara?

_____ flowers

---

4 Ana had 10¢. She got 8¢ more for cleaning the kitchen. How much money does she have altogether?

_____ ¢

---

5 Timmy had 20¢. He bought a pencil for 5¢ and a pen for 10¢. How much money does he have left?

_____ ¢

---

6 There are 17 books on three shelves. Four books are on the top shelf. There are 10 books on the middle shelf. How many books are on the bottom shelf?

_____ books

 Name

Super Problem Solver

Find the missing numbers.

1 ___ + 6 = 10

2 ___ – 4 = 6

Find each answer and write it on the line.

3 Juan had 3 toy cars. He got 2 more for his birthday. How many cars does he have altogether?

_____ cars

4 Mala's cat had 5 kittens. She gave 1 kitten to a friend. How many kittens does Mala have left?

_____ kittens

5 Tom bought 11 apples, 4 bananas, and 7 oranges at the store. How much fruit did he buy in all?

_____ pieces of fruit

6 Sara brought 20 cookies to the party. The children ate half of them. How many cookies are left now?

_____ cookies

FS122129 The Tutor's Handbook: Math Grade 1

Let's Review

Numbers and Computation
Solve.

1 3
   +2

2 12
    + 7

Circle the third teddy bear.

3

Patterns
Finish the patterns.

1 △ ☐ ☐ △ _____ _____

2

1	2	2	1	2			

3 50 ___ ___ 80 ___ 100

 Name

Let's Review

Geometry

Match the shapes.

a.

b.

c.

d.

Measurement

 How much money do you have?

_____ ¢

 Use a ruler to find the length.

_____ in.

 Name

Let's Review

Data Analysis

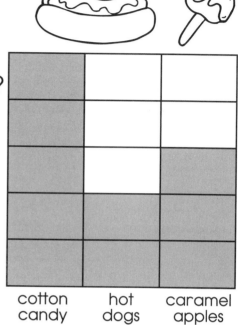

1 How many more caramel apples were sold than hot dogs?

_____

2 Which food sold the least?

_____

cotton candy	hot dogs	caramel apples

Problem Solving

1 Tomas invites 7 friends to his birthday party. His mom makes 10 cupcakes. How many will be left? (Don't forget to include Tomas.)

_____ cupcakes

2 Kenisha has 50¢. Troy has 20¢. How much money do they have altogether? Do they have enough to buy a candy bar that costs 60¢?

_____ ¢

yes   no

FS122129 The Tutor's Handbook: Math Grade 1

Student Survey

1 How much do you like math?

a little   some   a lot

2 How good are you at math?

not very good   OK   very good

3 Would you like to spend more time doing math?

no   maybe   yes

4 Do you understand math better now?

no   yes

5 What did you like best about tutoring?

_____

_____

6 What part of math do you need more help with?

_____

_____

Answers

Page 17
1. 10
2. 12
3. 5
4. 2
5. 15
6. 2
7. 10
8. 6, 12, 14
9. 15, 25, 30
10. 26

Page 18
1. 10
2. 14
3. 31, 34, 35
4. 90, 93, 94
5. 3 tens 1 one, 31
6. 5 tens 4 ones, 54

Page 19
2. 11, 11 − 4 = 7
3. 18, 18 − 9 = 9
5. 2, 3 + 2 = 5
6. 3, 5 + 3 = 8
11. <
12. >

Page 20
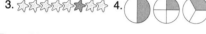
3. 4.

Page 21
1. 4
2. 12
3. 14
4. 11
5. 5
6. 3
7. 21
8. 19
9. 13
10. 12
11. <
12. >

Page 25
1. square, triangle, square
2. x, two squares
3. 5, 3, 4, 5
4. B A A B
5. 6, 10
6. 30, 35
7. 3 + 2 = 5   5 − 3 = 2   5 − 2 = 3

Page 26
1. circle
2. circle
3. triangle
4. square and triangle

Page 27
1. 3, 4
2. 4, 3
3. 10, 12, 14
4. 60, 70, 80
5. 20, 30
6. 75, 80, 85

Page 28
1. 3 + 1 = 4   1 + 3 = 4   4 − 3 = 1
   4 − 1 = 3
2. 7 + 8 = 15   8 + 7 = 15   15 − 7 = 8
   15 − 8 = 7
3. 6 + 5 = 11   5 + 6 = 11   11 − 5 = 6
   11 − 6 = 5
4. 4 + 9 = 13   9 + 4 = 13   13 − 9 = 4
   13 − 4 = 9

Page 29
1. square, triangle
2. diamond, square
3. 7, 8, 9
4. A B B
5. 45, 65, 75
6. 80, 110
9. 5 + 4 = 9   9 − 4 = 5   9 − 5 = 4

Page 33
1. 4
2. 6
3. 3
4. 4
5. d
6. c
7. a
8. b

Page 34
Student answers should replicate shapes given.

Page 35
1. gift box
2. soup can
3. globe
4. ice cream cone
5. ice cube

Page 36
1. 4
2. 5
3. 3
4. 4
5. 5
6. 3
7. 4
8. 6

Page 37
1. rectangle
2. triangle
3. cone
4. cube
5. 3
6. 5
7. ice cream cone

Page 41
1. top crayon green, bottom crayon purple
2. right brush green, left brush purple
3. 2 in.
4. 5 cm
5. 3:00
6. 9:30
7. 20¢
8. 66¢

Page 42
1. 5 cm
2. 7 cm
3. 2 in.
4. 3 in.
5. 9¢
6. 41¢

Page 43
1. November
2. 30
3. Saturday
4. Nov. 24
5. 5

Page 44
1. 10:00
2. 6:00
3. 8:00
4. d
5. a
6. b
7. c

Page 45
1. color bottom right pencil
2. 2 in.
3. 4 cm
4. 9:30
5. 18¢

Page 49
1. 4
2. 6
3. 3
4. 7
5. circles
6. squares
7. 3

Page 50
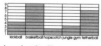
1. basketball
2. 2

Page 51
1. blue
2. 5, 1, 2
3. 1
4. 2

Page 52
1. 8
2. 7
3. March
4. February
5. 2

Page 53
1. dogs
2. birds
3. 4
4. 1
5. 3

Page 55
1. 8
2. 17
3. 3
4. 7
5. 14
6. 15

Page 56
1. 3, 8 − 5 = 3
2. 6, 10 − 4 = 6
3. 4, 15 − 11 = 4
4. 6, 9 − 3 = 6
5. 7, 5 + 2 = 7
6. 20, 12 + 8 = 20
7. 10, 4 + 6 = 10
8. 18, 8 + 10 = 18
9. 6
10. 2

Page 57
1. 5
2. 4
3. 7
4. $5.00
5. 7
6. 9

Page 58
1. 3
2. 7
3. 3
4. 18¢
5. 5¢
6. 3

Page 59
1. 4
2. 10
3. 5
4. 4 kittens
5. 22
6. 10

Page 60
Numbers and Computation
1. 5
2. 19
3.

Patterns
1. square, square
3. 2, 1, 2
3. 60, 70, 90,

Page 61
Geometry
1. c
2. d
3. b
4. a

Measurement
1. 87¢
2. 4 in.

Page 62
Data Analysis
1. 1
2. hot dogs

Problem Solving
1. 2
2. 70¢ yes

FS122129 The Tutor's Handbook: Math Grade 1